war{n}pieces

Leo Jenkins

DEAD RECKONING
20 17
COLLECTIVE

To you:
The mad ones
With holes in your chest
Broken and bleeding
Who gave your last breath
To laugh at death
Still believing
That dying for a
Fleeting triviality
Beats living
For nothing.

"And the best at murder are those who preach
against it

And the best at hate are those who preach love

And the best at war, finally, are those who
                              preach peace."

                                        -Charles Bukowski

Introduction

In lieu of an introduction to this collection
of poetry,
here is a story…

I knew this child. He came from a crumbling
love. He stood inquisitive on dirty knees, was
a master of climbing trees, and all things
sugary. He was sensitive for a little boy, not
enough to evoke concern in the father, just
enough to be misunderstood at times.

He loved the sound of rare desert rain
marching on tin and the smell of life which
preceded in the bloom of myriad wildflowers.

He hid himself from the storm of adolescence
in music. He hid himself from abuse, crawling
through dark rhythm in search of light like a
melody. He became not the song, but what the
song meant.
He could love no more than he had been loved.
He wrote beautifully about beauty with
contempt.

Those frustrating years he wandered in search
of a distant forgone crucible. His soft hands
held the answers, but could not lift the
questions. There was no bridge for boys like
him. There was no way to cross the ravine.
Until love came and gave a gift. Frustration
was love. Vengeance was love. War was love.
Killing was love. Dying was love.

So with those soft hands, the boy became a
man, building a bridge from flailing chunks of
flesh and bone. Through the arid, black night,
he stepped, not alone, but among the other
boys. The ones building, the ones destroying,
the ones building, the ones destroying, the
ones building. Each morning, they smiled at
one another through the gore of their love.
They smiled in unison at the bridge-builders
brotherhood. Some fell along the way, the
others promised to remember their names. They

called those boys heroes, who just wanted to be called men.

From the other side, he looked back and saw the inquisitive little boys walking on dirty knees, following. "This is not your bridge!" The man screamed. But it was too tempting, the boys wanted the same thing; to be complete, to transcend, to be men.

So with bloody hands, the man lifted his pen and then began. He sketched a subtle warning to the oncoming children about perspective. When he saw this was ineffective, he wrote a sign in bold letters, *THIS BRIDGE LEADS TO HARD ROADS THAT ONLY YOU WHO CROSS WILL KNOW*. The sign saved a few lives, but none from the other side. They were of the men who cried late at night, self-despised, for building bridges in the night.

The man grew older, writing desperately, warning songs in dark rhythm and light melody. Each one seemingly dividing him from who he used to be. While at the same time, keeping him there perpetually. He loved the children he never met. He wanted something better for them. But at that ravine, he could not forever stand. The road was long before him, the longest moment he sat in reflection. The path from war was winding through love to redemption. That was the bridge that would make him a man.

Time.
Time falls.
Time falls like the ash from burning bridges, obscuring vision.

Love.
Love calls.
Love calls through the darkness, the boy is now man enough to listen.

Here, here is what love told him…

What's Real

Though victory I cannot see,
I'm told we're heroes
You and me.
I'm told it wasn't murder
'Cause it happened overseas.
I'm told by those with hands clean,
"That's the way it's gotta be."

I told myself, start shedding
The pain and misery.

Our bones were made to break,
Forsake the suffering.
Bones were made to heal,
What's real is overcoming.

Invader G

I met a man while walking,
His clothes - ill-fitting.
Seemed he'd seen some hard times,
Seemed he'd crossed some fine lines,
To get to where he's going.

I met a man while walking,
          Our feet shuffled in the sand.
One of us on patrol,
The other, a late-night stroll,
          In midnight's holy land

I met a man while walking,
We engaged in culture's stare.
I hated him.
He hated me.
Now that's our cross to bear.

Six Feet

I was six feet from dying
The night, bleak and arid, still.
I was six feet from dying
Beneath a midnight moon's blue chill.
I was six feet from dying
On a routine outing to find, capture, or kill.
Found myself six feet from dying
Amid the bark of bending steel.
Few present moments now feel as real
As the night I was six feet from dying
Next to men accustomed to surviving
Such commonplace ordeal.

I.L.D

"Hmm." He said, curiously, as he thumbed
through my book.
"People aren't really rhyming in poetry these
days."
The thing now is to say something big
in a small way,
or better yet, to not say it at all,
tip-toeing the borders of a thought
in refugee slippers,
hushed and impervious to deportation
by old white men in jackets
with unnecessary elbow patches
or rabid feminists with coke bottle glasses
hidden behind rejection and suppressed
feelings of inferiority

who froth and frolic at obscurity,
bending back into itself
making a shadow from its own insides
then celebrating itself in a black tie.

Look, I'll take the "low brow" crowd
they're more fun to drink with, anyhow
they're proud and loud
and bob heads to the sound
of Wu-Tang Clan,
with stories about Afghanistan
that would blow your mind
like an
Improvised ~~Explosive~~ Literary Device

Frank Stanford Goes to War

Brother Leo told me the bell was ringing,
Since you can't keep a choir from singing,
          the ink bled like new beginnings.
I loomed out and saw them
Laid out like autumn.
One must die
          That others may live.
The metaphorical service
That nature is based in,
That others must die
For new life to thrive,
          The cycle of duty and purpose.

حُبّ

We broke
The sleeping
On rooftops
With rotor wash.

We ran
With death hands
In a land
Time forgot.

We shared
A moment
We loved,
We loved not.

15:3

The Lord is a man of war:
    The Lord is his name
The Lord is a man of war,
    lives he took away.

Truth Requires no Belief

I awoke in the wake
Of a neon dream
I saw myself
Hemorrhaging
Teeth biting clean
Remembering
Days of meaty grizzled
stumps pumping euphoria
Through midnight skies
And under the watchful eye
Of God's unpleasant truth,
We don't all grow old.

Said, My Father

Out of the Army, not a beard's worth of time.
Coerced dad into running a half-marathon with
me.
We were victorious in both having finished,
despite no training.
We cheered the day in solidarity of swollen
knees and triumphant experience.
We laughed together, joyfully.
The phone rang.
"Doc, it's so-and-so. Regan is… Regan was
killed in Iraq."
                    -4 days in bed-
Knowing I should have been there.
Said my father, "You're stronger than this."
Through tears, I replied, "I've lost my
purpose."
"Son, whatever you do, JUST DON'T DO NOTHING."
When the phone rings now, as it often does,
I'm just strong enough,
to lift a pen,
and not do nothing.

Destry

Wake up.
Put the coffee on.
Check the feed.
Another brother gone.
Grin through the grief,
The pain and suffering.
Daughter climbs onto my knee,
Requests a reading
Of Shel Silverstein.
It's becoming too familiar,
This mourning routine.

Share What You Can

"I drew a scene of a cat tap dancing."
"What do you mean?"
"What do you mean, what do I mean? It's a cat
tap dancing. His shoes are ruby red with
specks of green."
"What the fuck does that have to do with
anything?"
"Well, I didn't know how to draw
six men standing tall,
Before the blast, before the fall,
Of two fathers, six sons, a newborn ghost.
I can live those things in lucid dreams,
Second squad's alpha and bravo teams,
disappearing-
The displaced head of a man, mostly intact,
But I can't share all that, so here's a cat,
tap dancing,
His shoes are red and green."

Posthumous Self-Indulgent Inquiries in a Final Letter to You, Old Friend.

Was it the first time in a long time you felt warm? A blanket cascade of crimson life, on loan, returning. Fast at first, I'm sure, spurting. When the blood slowed, and the warmth turned cold, did you think of them? Your children? What a moment that must have been. Did you think you made a mistake? Knowing you can't reach down down down the drain and grab your life again. Cold now. Tired. Did you see the platelets struggling frantically, desperate to keep you together? Did life dry before your wet eyes? Did you know we all cared, no, we loved you and would have done anything to keep your life out of the drain. All of us, the strength, the resilience, what we would've done. Despite our vast reach, we still can't pull your living parts back up now. You're all mixed with piss and shit and shampoo and your daughter's long blonde hair that always clogged the drain. I know, you meant to take care of that last week but didn't get around to it. You were busy. Well, that's what you told us. Really you were in a crippling state of desperate depression, unnecessarily battling alone. We didn't know. You were "too strong" to let on. True strength is asking for help. That's why I don't understand, you were always the strong one — the one we admired. I hope you didn't see your life coating and staining that blonde hair you used to brush. I hope that didn't make you think about her first haircut or the time you were teaching her to ride her bike, and she fell off and got that scar on her forehead, the one you used to kiss every night as she fell asleep. No one to kiss away her pain now. I hope you didn't think of all that between the time you opened yourself and when your eyes closed the very last time.
Anyway, tell the other guys I said hello, I love them, and that we are all doing our best to take care of each of your daughters now.

                    With love and respect - your brother,
                                                      Doc

Accountability

Blame the mouth and tongue,
They're the ones who swallowed it.
Blame the mind that begged for ecstasy.
Blame the glass, the ice, the whiskey.
Blame a broken heart or endless war.
Just don't blame me.

The Marionette

Young men march
Like marionettes
While politicians
Place their bets,
A safe wager,
A pound of flesh
Torn from the backs
Of those marionettes.
And the vultures feast.
And the trumpets din.
Violent honor somehow
absolves the sin
Yet leaves the living
with regret
-so unfortunate-
To dress our children
As the marionette.

& The Pantoum Rolls On

...And the days pass on.
Long gone, yet forever sung
A cadence strong of Are's song
Which rolled right off the tongue.

Long gone, yet forever sung,
Our memories of blasphemies
Which rolled right off the tongue-
Onto the air, and in the ear, of a nation's
everyone.

Our memories of blasphemies
Is what we've now become,
Put on the air, into the ear, of a nation's
everyone.
Now we hear, so clear, our hero beat the drum.

Is that what we've now become-
Trading sacred spear and stone for gun?
Now we hear, so clear, our hero trade the
fiddle for the drum.
A choice becomes a lifetime's work to
overcome,

Trading spear and stone for sacred gun.
In these tribes, we survive the different ones.
A choice, a lifetime's work to overcome-
The sound we made with the beating, the
beating, the beating of that drum.

In these tribes, we survive the different ones.
With a sound profound-
The beating, the beating, the beating of the
drum!
While living together beneath the same dying
sun.

With a sound profound
We sing a cadence strong of Are's song
While dying together beneath the same living
sun
...and the days pass on.

<u>07JUN44</u>

The bodies are speechless,
Lay blissful bloody beaches.

<u>12SEP01-Foreseeable Future</u>

Our violence is silence
On repeat.
Drones overhead - in bed,
Haj don't sleep.

Villanelle's War

If what we gain is what we've lost
Would we spend a dollar more?
Had we known the final cost,

Would we those mighty oceans cross
To raid a foreign shore?
If what we gain is what we've lost,

What value have bodies by the tempest-tossed?
To test our virtue's core?
Had we known the final cost,

Those true and faithful few would still exhaust
Their minds upon this worthy chore.
If what we gain is what we've lost,

Make pen of sword and challenge Robert Frost,
Blood and ink to lessen burden bore.
Had we known the final cost,

Still, upon our skin, their names embossed,
We live on writing Villanelle's War.
What we gain is what we've lost.
Had we only known the final cost…

No Fury

Hell hath no fury,
I've looked her in the eyes-
One blue as the burgeoning day,
One dark as midnight skies.
I kissed her on her filthy mouth,
She bled back into mine.
Although it seems disturbing,
We still reminisce from time to time.

Hell hath no fury,
We took vacation there-
Not once or twice,
But most our life,
To learn what despair
there is to care.
Came back a man
To foreign lands
etched her name
In everything.

Hell hath no fury
Hell hath no fury
As the dream
Of leaving her
Will bring.

I: Took an Oath

I:
No gunslinger,
Nor Spartan
I:
No lion,
Nor gnashing jaws.
I:
No saint,
Nor servant
I:
No victim,
Nor entitled broken.
I
Know tragedy.
I
Know overcoming.

Looking Back in 20.20

Back in the day we use'ta kill terrorists
with steel-eyed looks from afar.

We recited Sylvia Plath and Emily Dickinson,
And the jihadists exploded before our eyes.

But the war marched on
And people began to shoot one another
With uncivilized bullets.

<u>Dear War,</u>

I'm tired of writing you. I'm tired of your late nights and wanton ways. I know I'm not the only one.

I won't speak for them, War, but I can't stand what you've done to my friends. Your seduction; some crucible, some adventure, some purpose, a rescue from the barren lands of adolescence. You, you fucked so many of them, War. I know it wasn't rape. Sorry I started that rumor. They dressed the part. They were asking for it. They knew what they were getting themselves into, after all — consenting adults, and so on, and such.

They stay up nights mulling you over. There's a new infection going around, you know. Or possibly an old one with a new name. So many of them think that they have it after being with you. I'm sure most of them don't. It's just so difficult being the only one left without a scar.

What's worse, War, you made them heroes. You made my friends bold - unafraid of death and consequence. If that wasn't bad enough, God damn it War, you went and made them strong. Then sent them back to the weak, who outnumbered them 200 to 1. I watched so many of them shrivel to those odds, begging. Begging for employment. Begging for acceptance. Begging for another opportunity to share their worthy experience for the greater good.

Please, War, don't get this bent. I don't resent you. After all, you made us men. After we were with you, our fathers shook our hands - looked us in the eye with pride.

Perhaps none of this is your fault, War. Perhaps all those Hollywood actors and poets and liberal arts majors and dead children have it wrong about you, War. Perhaps you're not so bad. Perhaps I'm being dramatic. Perhaps attacking you is just picking low hanging fruit, because, after all,

War, no one in their right mind likes you. But I need to remind you, you're way behind on rent.

War, five trillion, nine-hundred billion dollars and twenty-seven cents January 12th, 2019.

You've left your mess scattered like myriad broken families. What's worse, War, you spent our rent on shiny new trucks to compensate for your shitty personality. In fact, War, we've been paying your bills for so long we're past due on our student loans, health insurance policy, and credit card payments. And you still haven't done the fucking yard work like you promised. Now that I think about it, there seems to be more weeds around than when you arrived. Can't seem to be able to evict you, though. No matter how many shamans, shrinks, or bartenders we hire. There seems to be no getting rid of you, War. Will you at least do the fucking yard work?

War, do you remember that time… Never mind, no one is listening. They always ask about you, War. What you're really like. Did you know that about the others, the ones who never met you, the ones who never had to clean you from beneath their fingernails? You're so romantic to them. They make movies about you. They have special occasions to celebrate you. They even dress their children up like you, War. But then when you show up on their feed or on TV, they scroll past or change the channel. They're obsessed with you, War, as long as you're fucking someone else. Perhaps if they actually knew you, their movies would end differently. They're obsessed with you, but when I tell stories about you, War. They try to feed me pills. It's all so confusing.

War, the plum blossoms have fallen.

War, I loved you, with every ounce of my hate.

War, I read your story. The one written by the thorn of a Rose. He knew you well. He walked your lines with crisp eyes and a vigilant tongue, salivating at the chance to become a part of you, to know your insides, to get drunk with you and give you no more respect than you give yourself until you're laid out on regretful sheets in need of bleach crying, "No Joy!"

War, the tourniquets you made came in handy. We wrapped them around the necks of birthing mothers. How magnificent to witness life come from death.

War, you've been inside us before, but not this long. I think we may have an infection. May we borrow some of your antibiotics again? Look at me, asking you to heal a wound you created. It's not like you're a combat medic. Yes War, I'm being facetious again. Fuck you.

Am I rambling? Forgive me, War. I'm still learning how to function with this traumatic brain injury. Writing helps. So does marijuana. Not sure if I should thank you for that. The marijuana, not the rambling. I had no interest in the stuff before we met. It seems to ease the jagged parts of our encounters. Seems to help me sleep. Seems to still be illegal. You're still legal, though. Hallelujah.

War, what's it like to be declared? Is it validating? Men and women wearing four-thousand dollar suits, raising their hands in favor of you. Aren't they the same ones who keep avoiding you? Bone spurs are an affliction of the rich and powerful.

War, I observed the students debating you with such vigor. It was cute, War. The words they used - Dignified. If only they knew what you did last week while you were drunk, War. They might take off those silly red hats.

War, I'm tired of wearing you on my skin.

Goodbye.

Interactionism{with a pen}

The birds are conversing
        and I'm writing poetry.
The mountains peek out from behind the blue hue
of early morning
        and I'm writing poetry.
Spring slowly gains ground on winter, written in
cactus bloom and myriad migrating monarchs
        and I'm writing poetry.
A child holding technology grows into an
understanding of things like the world, and how
it works, and their place within it,
        and I'm writing poetry.
Day laborers in long sleeve shirts plunge their
hands into earthen mounds and withdraw taco
toppings, in the midday sun of Mexico
        and I'm writing poetry.
People protest for the right to speak, shot down
in the street, for using their words against a
tyrant.
        and I'm writing poetry.
The leader of the free world has a prolific
twitter presence.
        and I'm writing poetry.
On the wall of a bar, a flatscreen television
plays a sporting event with 30-second
advertisements that cost enough to feed a small
country. The people cheer.
        and I'm writing poetry.
The American war in Afghanistan against a
malleable ideology has been ongoing for two
decades, at the cost of over 150,000 lives and
$2,000,000,000,000 because 15 Saudi Arabians, 2
Emiratis, an Egyptian, and a Lebanese were
glutinous on the fruit of religious belief, fed
to them by a now deceased, wealthy Saudi Arabian
brat and a political extremist Egyptian doctor.
        and I'm writing poetry.
This planet has four-thousand, two-hundred
religions. This solar system has 8 planets and 1
star. There are 100 thousand million stars in
this galaxy alone, and 100 billion galaxies in
the known universe.
        and I'm writing poetry...
                                What else to do?

Reflections from a Lumberjack

How can it be
Humanity waged war
Against the tree
And never took a single casualty?
Built homes from their corpses.
Shoulda used that strategy
Against the Iraqi,
Instead, we drop bombs of confetti.
Instead, we invoke diplomacy.
When we should'a made planks from their
bodies, savagely.
Then used cameras to our advantage
To construct our own reality.
We shoulda preached necessity
On TV
Of burning their saplings.
If you're gonna kill ruthlessly
Do it completely...
Or don't do it at all.

NeurotiCatharticA

Give me something to write with
Then fuck off out the door.
Give me something to write with;
The pain I've felt before,
The rage from better days,
And all our memories of war.
Get me something to write with,
I'll share some sins with you.
Their burden names are guilt and shame
Etched upon my skin, turned blue.
Now get me something to write with,
A bottle full or empty memory will do.
Just make it strong,
The night is long,
And the release is overdue.

If it's some disease that spills me
I'll come clean at my ending.
BUT
If it's something breathing that kills me
I'm taking 'em with me

Raging and Screaming

Pray for Peace, Prepare...

I hope war is what you wanted.
I hope pain is what you had in mind.
Now the suffering is upon you,
And not all wars end with time.
Now you're asking for the suffering,
Grasping at what's mine.
Now you're choking on the suffering,
And I'm breathing here just fine.

All Bleeding Eventually Stops

A mind on fire,
frantic.
Still night air
Clutching cold despair.
Smoldering.
Waking in ash of past
Memories,
And not so pleasant
Present dependencies.
Escaping dead evenings
In nicotine.
Mourning mornings
Brought back ourselves
Clever caffeine, cascading.
Black river, hither, forever flowing,
Molding
A heart-shaped stone.
Knowing
All flames eventually succumb,
Become numb,
And cease their burning.

<u>Disposition</u>

Your words will never make a difference
Until you point them in the right direction.
Your love will never come to fruition
In this arid wasteland.
Your clenched heart hits like a fist
With collateral devastation,
And your demons will run you
until you learn to embrace them.
But the whiskey don't listen,
      just hastens this disposition.

Face{mask}Yourself

If I were a lyric
I'd be Lars Ulrich-
Arrogant and repetitive.

If I were a sedative
You could pour me over ice
At first, I'd be nice.

But would tear you apart in the morning.

If I were news
I'd be a hurricane warning.

And if I were like the rest of them
I'd be pretty damn boring.

But if I were a virus,
I'd conspire to remind us,
Everything breathing dies.
Nothing living survives.
Stop acting surprised
And live your life.

See Title Below

Locked down, shut in.
So frantic without motion,
Started throwing water
At the ocean.
Been selling devotion
To pay interest on debts
I don't have yet.
Been trapped behind
A set of rules designed
For applauding fools
Happy gagged, surrendering.
politicians pandering,
Slandering liberty.
Been avoiding social completely,
Neatly organizing the plastic
Avoiding spastic toddler tantrums
When they say, "she can't come in."
Gotta grin when
I hear it said again
Free at last, free at last
Thank the government almighty
Thank the poor
Thank the tiny
Thank the dead and dying
Thank the homeless pushing carts
Thank the low prices at Walmart
Thank the world's first trillionaire
Thank the structure that put him there
Thank the home delivery
Of Fact and Memory
Thank the books that read us
"Freedom's History."

you{we}me

These things these things
these beautiful things,
these broken edges
and tattered seems
of egalitarian dreams
we dreamed
we dreamed
we woke and screamed
when fear seamed
to be our new reality,
this looming melancholy
dividing "we"
into you and me
splitting a tree of liberty
who gave its leaves
for centuries
shading mostly me.

How devastating, these things
these things, these just dreams
we dreamed.

Could this be
an awakening –
a systematic oppression ending?
or transforming?
or is this a warning,
from the "we"
to the powers that be?
But the powers that be
are still part of we.
Can't stress this enough,
the true strength
of a people is solidarity.
We stand divided
yet lay united,
gasping desperately,
'Cause if you can't breathe,
We can't breathe.

What's Heard

I have a friend named Alex
Who works in federal law enforcement.
We go surfing,
We talk about things
Like our favorite memes
And what it means
To be American.
We differ as often
As we agree,
I listen to him,
He listens to me;
Diatribes about LSD
And breaking the law
Unmercifully.
The point I made
On anarchy, he
Politely disagreed.
The stance he took
On use of force
Helped me to see
Things differently.
We share concern
For our country
A place we love
A free we need.
Neither press,
We both conceded
Poor leadership
Is devastating.
A perfect storm
Is forming,
Partially born of forlorn
Opinions flapping, formed
From those lacking
Experience, education, and otherwise
Not surprised
We were born of rebellion,
Throwing tea at the ocean,
Splintered in factions
Fractions of power divided
It's how the experiment survived
We thrived in the hard times
Defined by weight we carried
Not party lines.

Defined by friendships
Not petty crimes.

The burden of freedom
Burgeons in conversational narrative.
What's said is important,
What's heard is imperative.

So we talk.
We listen,
We laugh,
We reminisce then
We wish the other well,
                    And mean it.

777.1
or
To Be Here

Maybe I'm making mountains
Out of metaphors,
Morphing fear of foreign culture
Into another winless war,
Burning bones of dinosaurs
Shipping needless goods
From exploited distant shores.

Perchance, I'm being dramatic
About the amygdala gone spastic,
Media beats that button
Ignores an ocean filled with plastic.
Laws ban mind-expanding psychedelics.
Corporations procure profits
Promoting fun-loving alcoholics.

Could it be, I'm being silly
Making mention of a planet
Becoming progressively less chilly
Or resources collected involuntarily
And spent unethically
While children go hungry.
I'm open to the possibility
That I'm just lucky

To be here.

Poetics and Rhetoric

I keep writing lines,
  But nothing fits.
That's what I get
  For mixing poetry and politics.
  Aristotle sold Rhetoric,
But there ain't a dime
  In heroic couplets.
  Just as well,

        This is no hero and
  I'm not for sale.

Two Simple Things

Left wing - right wing
          {of the same dying bird}
Flapping - blaming
Accusing - labeling
the other wing
Intolerant...
Doesn't just happen in politics
It's in every argument.
It's the way we are on the internet.
It's the way we hedge our bets
guarding opinions, we haven't challenged yet.
You're wrong,
'Cause I'm right.
They're too uptight
About the past,
I believe in change
And want it fast.
I believe in freedom.
I believe in safety.
I believe in human.
I believe in me.
I see you there,
Guarding your fear,
The weapons you wield,
Throwing guilt like a spear
Using shame like a shield.
I see you there,
Attempting to steer
The conversation
In another direction.
I see you there
Building a straw man
To defend your castle in the sand.
I hear you, please hear me
Listening is what we need
Please, please believe
these two simple things:
                {Listening is what we need}
We are the bird
          Not its wings.

I think too much

I think about people
        Spending time, in line,
Buying things.
And I think about the wisdom
That poverty brings.
And I dream
A daytime dream, intoxicating.
From a circle pit of demons
I'm watching
Better angels sing
A song about belonging,
A rhyme regarding
The sin in me
broken free,
And a rhythm in motion
Toward ultimate complexity.
        And some line out of time,
About eternity.
Could it be,

                                I think too much?

What's your take on Theoretical Physics?

With no propriety
Within society
        The artist spreads their wings
        Investigating ethereal things,
        A theory of strings
Interconnecting inter-dimensional
        beings,
In plural prose
        Or multiverse,
The truth is tiny
        The truth is sparse.

Do you follow?

        Do you lead?

Do you realize,
        It's the same damn thing?

We, the Wheel

You create the lie you're told
What to buy sold by I
And other friends in tow,
I bought these shares with time
Waiting in line for my funeral.
Commodity is you and me
tech farmers planting seeds-
Data harvesting.

I bought the shares you sold.
I ate your weight in gold
Precious metal < Precious moments.
Deactivate, realign the focus-
Lenses, filters, blur emotions.
Screens on streams of dopamine,
Never felt so hopeless,
Yet simultaneous self-awareness
Of being so self-important.

What lurks beneath the surface
Of that stream is apathy,
{An undertow}
Receding humanity
Receiving calamity with coffee;
Repeating, repeating, repeating
What we seem to be buying
In bulk,
In droves,
With moments
Like spokes
Attached, we the wheel,
Rolling.
No breaks.
No way of knowing
Where we're going,
Or who we will be
When we arrive.
Just scratching an itch
Comprised of a scratch
That's making us itch,
Still buying, still selling
Stilling dying to live
Still breathing like apes
In a cave with all this;

With fear of what's
Out there, getting in,
With needs like the rain
And the sun on our skin.
We, the ones drinking
The apathy.
We, the ones so desperately
In need of empathy.
We, the ones whose hands
Built weaponry
To overcome the fear
Of what's out there
{getting in}
We, whose thumbs have been
Busy building weaponry
Now click them up
To shift the weight of poverty,
To support the hungry,
The dead and dying.
But our thumbs must be broken,
These token gestures
Just ain't working.

Could it be time to realign
And focus on what's lurking
Beneath the surface,
Or shall we make
                    Another purchase?

Text Messages to Nick Cahill

Do you know
The cost of citrus
in the snow?
A dollar a lime,
Two for an avocado.
Sure, it's a long way to go
Over borders
Undertows
Currents of trade expose
The cost of fuel,
The value of bones.
Fossils aren't cheap
And neither are those
Tiny limes or avocados.

What about tequila tho?
Made by hands
Attached to souls
Receiving pennies
For dollars pulled
From pockets stitched
Into designer clothes
Made by hands
Attached to souls
Receiving pennies
For dollars pulled
from pockets, they stitched
Into those
designer clothes.

Titles are for Royalty, I'm just a poem.

Begging for change
Sure feels strange
When your tank ain't empty

But fuel still ain't free
And neither is prosperity.

Time is Free

Time is as free
As the air you breathe.
Time is a seed
With no need
For watering.
There's no cause for toil
Just place it in the soil...
And breathe.

Another Death Sentence

Did you hear
About fear
Being a liar?
Convicted on charges
To conspire;
To wheel and deal,
And try to steal,
Hope from desire.

What if

What if…
Cows liked being milked?
What if…
There's actually seven genders?
What if…

What if
We could disagree, respectfully?
What if
Death tastes like cotton candy?
What if
Life has no meaning, and we're all just
arguing over nothing?
What if
Sheep dreamed of counting shepherds?
What if sloths moved as fast as leopards?
        My God that would be terrifying!
What if
This squabbling was designed,
To keep us in line?
What if
It was sublime to be kind
What if…

What if
war 'n peace were pieces of the same thing?
Wow, now wouldn't that be something?

war{n}pieces

There are pieces of me
I've kept unseen;
Frayed and crumbling.
Shy - hiding behind
A thin veil of serenity.

They're not agony,
Nor world ending,
Or a soul torn in two.
They're heavy, that's true.
But they're nothing new.

They grind like rusty knees
And bleed
In the dark, empty spaces
In between
Expectations and suffering.

Internal relics worth remembering
The days before surrendering.
Surrounded by better men,
Whose parts misshapen saved them.
Whose war didn't betray them,
It made them.

Those parts remained contained
until the day she came
She peered through me,
Deep into my creases.
"What beauty," she said,
"In your war{n}pieces."

The Story of Strength in Reverse

The words rattled when he spoke,
Crackled in his throat,
He said, "I got nothing left."
She said, "If you've got a dying breath,
You've got a breath!
You've got something left!"
And her eyes told the story of strength
In reverse.
First,
-Unwavering conviction.
Then
-Calloused hands holding his broken.
-10,000 unseen steps; Mastering fear and
regret.
-Tears that fall like soldiers in the
forgotten dust of time and sacrifice.
-Forgiveness.
-Screaming, trembling razor lips, pressing hot
venom into the softest parts of their union.
-Uncertainty. Insecurity.
-Severed, unspoken expectations.
-Laughter and exploration.
-Soft hands gliding over warm skin.
-"Hello. I noticed you standing alone."

Defining

War is a drug that takes you.
Love is a smile that breaks you.
Poetry is the cadence of emotion.
Peace is a rowboat,
Redemption's an ocean.

Seven Layers of High Art

Seven layers of epiphany
Scatter the expanding sky.
The mountains reached their greedy peaks
To seize her warmth,
Finding only desolate desert beyond the stars.
Finding only hollow words disguised
As high art.

Action & Consequence

Chaos wrapped in harmony
Spontaneous still truth
Or madness
Prevailing light echos color
A warm summer day
A sunburnt night
Spent tossing and turning
To the rhythm
The alchemy
Of action and consequence

Coffee & Cigarettes

Coffee and cigarettes
As good as life gets
Made all the better
When we enjoy them together…
        But you don't drink coffee,
        And I don't like cigarettes.

Overdue Departures

The wind betrayed our skin that sultry summer
night-
Not strong enough to move the curtains,
Let alone our love.
So we lay atop sheets stitched from the thread
of overdue departures.
We lay separated by concrete and wires.
We lay distant, together. Silent.
      Waiting
For the crickets to finish their serenade
      Hoping
They play our song before it's too late.

The City {drowning} in the Sea

The color before the rain rang dying at her feet-
The sound, a common song sung, pierced deep.
Depart, descend, transcend the leaving
The sound before the rain became epiphany
words without meaning,
Painting skies unholy,
Purified before the endless dawn.
In waking, the shame of every unanswered drop
crushing the innocent pedals of guilty
flowers,
bending stalks etched in earth
An entitled forest, in lust, consuming.
The deluge, not enough to set the blossom
blooming.

The strong man hacks at the heavens,
dulling bone without regret
Drowning in consequence.
Blistered hands break.
Blood and rust, find mud and dust,
clay forms.
Eyes fixed on a living storm.
Clay forms, around the feet.
One eye breaks the sky in two,
Parting, departing, heaven born anew.

One-hundred-million years of deafening light
One-hundred-thousand breaths
One moment of attentiveness,
broken
Now beneath one-hundred-million years of clay,
turned stone,
a fossil flower still struggles to thank the
bone.
Perhaps one touch will undo the suffering,
The lust which brought the rain.
One gentle phrase, unspoken.
One endless dance between the maker, the
breaker,
                                    and the broken.

Love{less}

Love can not exist in a place with no empathy.
Love can not exist in a space with no honesty.
Love can not exist when it's cheaper than an
Apology.
So I'm calling bullshit.
Love outweighs pride, but the scales have
Tipped.
Love, you say, is infinite?
Then why is yours so delicate?
And why am I surprised
To be trivialized,
Sharing pain to your backside
While you speak of love
Like it's a free ride.
Like, once you claim it,
Well, that's it.
But love can't stand a hypocrite.
Love knows the difference
Between indifference and counterfeit
And love's not impressed when you're faking
It.

And neither was she.

Slings and arrows
Arrows and slings
These are a few of my favorite things;
Jazz on angel's wings,
Copulating on rusty bedsprings,
Dings in old trucks,
Being down, out-a-luck.
In love
Finding new ways to make a buck
Then finding a reason to give it up
       Then reach for the door
        'cause there's nothing more
Depressing
Than old bed springs
And mending
wounds from
        Arrows and slings.

It's tough

You know, it's tough
To be the better person
In handcuffs.
And it's tough
To say I forgive
When the rounds
Are still flying.
And it's tough
To see you crying
But not as tough
As reconciling
Losing a love
That's been defining,
Over pride
Under skin
Itching and bleeding
Picking scabs from within.
Wrists infected,
Sore to the touch,
Bound by the sound
Of ego's handcuffs.

Better Angels

We found serenity
In nudity,
And becoming self-aware.
Stepped into ourselves,
Through ourselves,
To find the other side.
The place where
Better angels cried.
They came alive
And envied you and I.
We watched in wonder and realized,
Ours was always the greener side.

She

She,
The mover of dreams;
In the light,
And in the night,
And in between.
She
Was made of
Impossible things,
Darkness that's bright
And dancing despite
The ache that morning brings.

Make

We made love
Like art
In the shadow of a broken forever

But not before
We stepped from war
And all its storied splendor.

Never Forget

In love, we fell
Like two towers,
Burning, crumbling.
Like silence of solitude shattered.
In love, we rose,
Like a nation.
Unity born of agony,
Like the old gift of living, resurrected.
In love, we see, blind,
Like the blessed.
No color, no politics,
Like unconditionally, "Never Forgets."
We made love
Like a slogan,
Carved it on the everywhere,
Like fear, like time doesn't own us all.
We remembered love
Like burning, crumbling, and agony.
The other parts went dormant
Like living, resurrection, and unity...

Until the next time, we fall.

We Are One

Terrified by some gleaming
Premonition of life leaving
This feeble shell still breathing
Around a broken mind still needing
The sanctity of believing
That we are one
We are one
We are one
Inseparable being.

Bean

Not
the ease a Sunday morning brings
Or
A quiet cup of coffee in the dawn of early spring.
Nor
A home that's always clean
Or
The enticing lights of Saturday nights, shimmering.
Not
                the road to something new
Or
                sleeping when I want to
No,
I don't miss a thing,
                        Whenever I'm with you.

Free.Choice

I
choose to live
forget and forgive
Him
for sin and
feign division
lest
we forget
begrudge and lament
love
like it came from
above
and through us
on its way to build
trust
in unity of all
things before and beyond
when

I choose to live

not simply survive
on a lie
made of time
I choose to die
at a moment all mine
enduring paradigm end
suffering
believing a part
of being
is choosing
to live

A Love Like Psychedelic

There was adoration in her eyes - a spark like
silence dancing naked in front of a mirror -
her tongue tasting the way it should, like
honey, like lies, like a swarm of bees after
the honey. Those soft fingers untangling the
hard knot that constricted us - those hard
hands constricting the soft parts of us. It
went on like this for hours, for seven
lifetimes.

The colors rose and fell and became aware of
the moonlight dancing on shadows from the
future.

She breathed into us one last time, shed a
hard tear from her eye to mine, and we
collapsed within each other at the dying light
of dawn when the drugs fell off, and all we
were left with was ourselves, entwined in the
memory of tomorrow, blinded by forever.

Tiny Poem

Tiny hands hold tiny pens writing tiny poems
for tiny books to sit on tiny shelves in tiny
homes
filled with tiny arguments over tiny problems
made of tiny ash scattered across a tiny
timeline
where we fight tiny wars with tiny bombs
while other tiny people sing tiny songs
about tiny houses and tiny cars
with tiny windows exposing tiny scars
made by tiny moments that form tiny bars
around tiny minds
molded by tiny teachers etching on tiny cards
some tiny numbers reminding us how tiny we
are.

Tiny alarm clocks make tiny noises
to get us early to tiny jobs
to earn tiny money to buy tiny shoes
for tiny feet to take tiny steps
down tiny roads through
tiny cities flooded with
tiny voices sharing tiny opinions
on tiny cell phones, during tiny calls,
all
to make tiny people feel tall.

Tiny bows on tiny boats
float on tiny oceans
bought with tiny fortunes
filling tiny expectations to keep up with the
Jones'.
While sticking up tiny noses
At tiny roses
grown in tiny gardens
hardened by tiny hail which fell
from tiny clouds housing tiny gods
commanding tiny legions of tiny cogs
who manufacture tiny debt
to coerce tiny servants to push tiny spokes
attached to tiny rims rolling over tiny
cultures
comprised of other tiny servants.

Tiny pigment in tiny cells
Tell us nothing about ourselves.

Tiny genders bicker about tiny stalls
in tiny bathrooms of tiny malls
Where tiny shoppers purchase tiny objects to
wrap in tiny paper
and place under tiny trees
upholding tiny traditions
of tiny religions
Helpless against tiny laps around a tiny dying
star.

Tiny moments
Tiny years
Tiny headlines
Tiny fears

Tiny dreams

Tiny breaths

Tiny lives

Tiny deaths

We are so tiny.

We are all so fucking TINY…

                         without love.

Bring US Home

Tempting brazen hearts with possibility
Deconstructing self-perceived inferiority
Through gaping mental holes construct
A new perennial reality.

Parting seas of these
Egregious opportunities
With flame to fall
Let's burn it all
And embrace the sprouting beauty.

Bring us home.

Realign the moon to shine
On everything that's mine,
Becoming yours
And all that burns with time.

Parting seas of these
egregious opportunities
With flame to fall
We burnt it all
Now let's embrace the sprouting beauty.

Bring us home
Bring us home
Bring
Us
Home.

Redemption Road

Redemption road is long, winding, and seldom
paved. We stumble. We fall. We learn to step
softly with grace through the broken edges of
ourselves. Steep, climbing on hands and knees,
bleeding we seep to soil, becoming one. All
the while terrified, knowing that at any time
our one solid handhold may give way causing an
avalanche sending us back to the start - no
shovel or rope or friendly set of eyes to dig
us out. Tread lightly. Black ice forms in the
shadowy corners of fear, apprehension, and
self-doubt. Traction is a moment unseen,
believing.
Step. Step.
One more dying step over bridges built in
earthquakes. Simple moments resting tired
legs, permit burning eyes to feed the belief
that this path, like our pain, is sempiternal.
Step. Step.
This life is long, winding, and seldom paved.
Step. Step...

About the Author

Leo Jenkins is the guy who wrote this.

He is also the author of Lest We Forget: A Ranger Medic's Story, On Assimilation, First Train out of Denver, With a Pen, and countless bathroom stall limericks.

Additionally, Leo is the creator and editor of a poetry anthology series that seeks to publish the work of military veterans, also published by Dead Reckoning Collective.

Acknowledgments

Thank you, David Rose.

"If I offended you, you needed it."
Corey Taylor

<u>Forthcoming Books</u>

War… &After: The Anthology of Poet Warriors

Lucky Joe

Addvice

COLLECTIVE

About the Publisher

Dead Reckoning Collective is a veteran-owned and operated publishing company. Our mission encourages literacy as a component of a positive lifestyle. Although DRC only publishes military veterans' written work, the intention of closing the divide between civilians and veterans is held in the highest regard. By sharing these stories, we hope that we can help clarify how veterans should be viewed by the public and how veterans should view themselves.

Visit us at

deadreckoningco.com

Facebook: @deadreckoningco
Instagram: @deadreckoningcollective
Twitter: @dr_collective

One Day in San Jose

Upon arriving - narrow streets broaden
horizons.
Redbrick decor at war
with progress, like a protest
from a time before.

Cafes boasting roasting beans, beckoning.
A door opens in front of me
leading to a garden green,
where short white cups filled with energy,
{sans calorie} entice productivity,
a proclivity apparently transcending
nationality.

The low hum of conversation
and spoons clanking porcelain
blend into the soundtrack of wind rustling
leaves of the evergreen canopy
shading tables filled with eggs and coffee;
while mangos hang like effigies
in memory of food wrapped in skin, not
plastic.

It's sounding more like day is here.
Shopkeepers unfurl their wares;
trinkets and hammocks,
novelty hats and cheap sunglasses.
And painkillers, painkillers, painkillers
galore!
          {How much pain are we in?}
What's more;
diet pills, sleeping pills, dick pills, and
Ritalin.
Cut out the middleman,
go straight to the source -
no doctor, of course,
it's cash only at each
          PHARMACY, PHARMACY, PHARMACY!
as far, as far as the eye can see,
enticing crispy,
fat gringos whose nose
point high, avoiding the eye
of each shopkeep, they pass by.

An inner voice is telling me,
compelling me to move,
to find another view.
So at a leisurely pace,
I head for the base
of the red and white tower
on top of the hill.

The old stone wall
has seen it all;
the rise and fall
of buildings,
hopes and dreams,
hurricanes pressing
palm tree leaves
above rooftops.
Bandits disguised as cops,
shaking down
both white and brown.

In a city made pretty
by pride and unity,
it seems there's
even more to see.
While the view seems pristine
perched high on the hill,
it lacks something simple,
I'm longing to feel.
From here I just see the buildings
not the people who built them,
and the structures confining,
not the humans trapped within them.

Crossing these roads begins a tale of two
cities.

The dogs get skinnier with each block I
descend.
I can see what's feeding them;
trash and broken glass
surrounded by rusted rebar and wire,
concrete and tin, and an old truck tire.
People get nervous to see a face they don't
know,
this is the same all over the world.

A few steps, a few turns...
Past the pain killers,
local vendors sell authenticity,
in the form of fresh fruit, fish, and
vegetables.
Three men in pointy boots
serenade patrons with guitar and accordion
blues.
Pristine white hats atop sweating brow,
singing the song of the proud *Vaquero.*

So compelled by the smells and the sights,
I lift my pen and begin to write...

Menudo and mole,
sopes y flautas
chiles rellenos
the fragrance surrounds us.

Mariscos, arroz
and huevos rancheros
for me it's the classic,
tacos dorados.

The fan runs full blast
to keep the moscas at bay
I can hear the men talk
don't know what they say.

the table communal
come one, come all
pour salsa on beans
that could take paint off the wall.

I pay the four dollars
to la cocinera maria.
So happy I found
this backstreet Loncheria.

As the day ends
and the night begins,
the sun fades away
while the moon ascends
and I find myself again
at the place where I began.

In the square, a family gathers
Around a beating drum;
the youngest one,
a girl of five,
dancing while grandma
keeps the beat alive.
Ancient shells 'round ankles.
The circle grows, and recedes,
like the seas,
like the joy and agony in me.

Twin pillars of faith,
each with a cross to bear
overlook the city square
        where gossip bleeds to culture.
Open doors for the willing,
commence the storytelling
of righteous killing,
in the name of love,
in the name of HIM.

Salvation is belief.
If it saves you,
say I,
"believe."

        Believe in Krishna, Vishnu, Shiva, or Jesus.
        Or the patron saint who ends your diseases.
                Pray to Osiris, Athena, or Isis.
        Pray to Hades or Satan for more spicy vices.
            Believe the Anunnaki, Abassi, or Buddah.
            Believe in Muhammad, or Odin and Frigga.
    Believe in all of ancient Greece's collective
                                            myths,
                    Or Chin the moon goddess,
            representing the power of female
                                destructiveness.
        Believe in a shape. Believe in the weather.
    Believe in yourself when it makes you better.

                                    As for me,
                    I pray to the "Big G" directly,
            the one perpetually touching humanity,
                the one who transcends eternity,
            who shaped the planets near and far,
                                    the stars,

                    and makes time a triviality.
                       If you're asking me,
                          I pray to gravity.

Back in the square,
in the dead night air
Patriotic harmony flickers
in celebration of independence,
and oversees a gathering
of freedom's fortunate descendants.

A toddler walks proud,
denying his father's hand,
insisting this road, he'll cross on his own.
The father just laughs,
perhaps remembering his father long ago.
Stubborn sons, never seem to learn,
until well after they're grown
and have stubborn children all their own.

Warm Tecates
wash down *tamales*,
Sitting, cerveza in hand,
on the steps of the San Jose Mission,
I heard the benediction
and then I had a vision

          I woke in the wake of a neon dream
            Phoenix Rising - Eyes opening;
          I saw the ways we could have been,
         A world deprived the war drum's din,
         A humanity free from the fable of sin,
                Enuk in circle center
              telling a story of *Origin*.

When I came to

And when the night found its end, I raised the
moon past half staff, beyond loves past, above
the last of our suffering days, beyond the
aching, beyond the pain. We hoisted to heavens
her body and openly embraced her name. All
before I watched the proud cripple hobble
away, through the simple town square in old
San Jose.

CPSIA information can be obtained
at www.ICGtesting.com
Printed in the USA
LVHW090311041120
670659LV00004B/229